Your Amazing Itty Bitty™ Police Wife Survival Guide

15 "Police Tips" for Navigating a Thriving Police and First Responder Marriage

Vikki Downey

Published by Itty Bitty™ Publishing
A subsidiary of S & P Productions, Inc.

Copyright © 2024

All rights reserved. No part of this book may be reproduced or transmitted in any form or by any means, electronic or mechanical, including photocopying, recording, or by any information storage and retrieval system without written permission of the publisher, except for the inclusion of brief quotations in a review.

Printed in the United States of America

Itty Bitty Publishing
311 Main Street, Suite D
El Segundo, CA 90245
(310) 640-8885

ISBN: 978-1-7322946-3-9

This information is for educational purposes only and is not intended as a substitute for medical advice, diagnosis, or treatment. You should not use this information to diagnose or treat a health or mental health problem or condition. Always check with your doctor before changing your diet, altering your sleep habits, taking supplements, or starting a new fitness routine. In addition, this book does not offer any legal, financial, or tax advice. Seek the advice of an attorney, a CPA, or a fee-only financial advisor if such service is needed.

Your Amazing Itty Bitty™ Police Wife Survival Guide

15 "Police Tips" for Navigating a Thriving Police and First Responder Marriage

The life of a police wife or first responder spouse is something most people don't think of. They live in an inordinate amount of continual stress. They must be supportive, understanding and stoic. They must protect their children from their own fears. They must navigate how the world sees them and educate friends and family about safety matters.

In her book, Vikki Downey, through her own experience, provides you with 15 tips to help you navigate the challenges of being a policeman's wife or first responder spouse and leverage a side business to reclaim your officer's time.

You will learn:

- What to expect as a policeman's wife or first responder spouse
- How best to support him
- How to survive night and overtime shifts
- How to navigate the way the world sees him
- How to Find family time along with self-care time

If You are the spouse of a policeman or know someone who is pick up a copy of this informative Itty Bitty™ Book today!

Dedication

This book is a tribute to my husband John and our two incredible children, Misa and John, who are adults now. As we embarked on this journey as a united family, we not only discovered the strength within ourselves but also forged an unbreakable bond that carried us through every challenge and every victory. Together, we were the unyielding four musketeers standing side-by-side.

I extend this dedication to the remarkable individuals across the globe who don the uniform and badge every day, venturing out to safeguard complete strangers, all while leaving their own families behind. It's a testament to their unwavering commitment to the service of others, a calling that carries them through each moment of uncertainty. Amidst the risks they face, the men and women in blue stand as the unsung heroes of our world. Your sacrifice and valor does not go unnoticed. From the depths of my heart, thank you for the immeasurable contributions to our world that you make each day.

Romans 13:4, NIV: "For the one in authority is God's servant for your good."

Stop by our Itty Bitty® website to find interesting blog entries regarding Police Officer Spouses.

www.IttyBittyPublishing.com

Or

visit Vikki Downey at

www.johnandvikki.com

www.vikkidowney.com

www.cleanmeetsperformance.com

Email Vikki at thevikkidowney@gmail.com for your **FREE GIFT:** Police Wife Workbook ~ Create Time and Financial Independence for Your Police Family.

Table of Contents

Introduction
Tip 1. What Most People Don't Know About Being a Police Wife
Tip 2. What To Expect as a Police Wife Through the Years
Tip 3. How You Can Best Support Your Police Hubby and Feel Supported by Him
Tip 4. You Will Raise Incredible Children in Your Blue Family Using These Ideas
Tip 5. Faith and Marriage Challenges
Tip 6. Understanding How the World Sees Your Husband
Tip 7. Educating Friends and Family About Important Safety Matters
Tip 8. What the World Doesn't Know About Your Husband
Tip 9. Surviving Night and Overtime Shifts
Tip 10. Surviving the Most Important Family Holidays Without Him
Tip 11. How to Stop Feeling at Times Like a Divorcee
Tip 12. Leveraging a Side Business to Reclaim Your Officer's Time
Tip 13. How to Build Up Your Husband When the Job Begins to Tear Him Down
Tip 14. Prioritizing Your Buddy and Girlfriend Time
Tip 15. Fulfilling Your Dreams Before and During Retirement

Introduction

This heartfelt book is the culmination of a 25-year journey, born from Vikki's experiences as a devoted police wife. In 1994, when her husband John made the life-altering decision to transition from owner of a successful automotive accessory business started at age 16, to police officer at 30, life took an unforeseen turn. At the time, their family included two young children, daughter Misa, age 4, and son John, age 3. With little prior exposure to the world of law enforcement, they embarked on this new path together.

Throughout the years, Vikki and John have learned and grown immeasurably. Many of their closest friends, impressed by Vikki's resilience and unique perspective, have persistently urged her to share their journey in the written word.

Now after much reflection, Vikki is ready to share her story, offering a beacon of support and encouragement to those in a similar situation. With a huge desire to help and guide fellow police wives who may feel isolated, she envisioned a short, comprehensive life and marriage guide to provide invaluable tips and insights to help navigate the demands of this exceptional calling. Whether it's deeper appreciation for sacrifices made or simply discovering the strength of the human spirit in the face of adversity, this book is a captivating and enlightening read.

Police Tip 1
What Most People Don't Know About Being a Police Wife

Whether you married a man who was already a police officer, or he joined his department or agency after you were already married, you play an important role as his partner in life. You are his ride-or-die mate. Always remember the following key points:

1. He needs to know you have his six (police jargon for back).
2. Despite some sleepless nights, you need to keep a great attitude.
3. He will often have to stay late writing reports or making late arrests.
4. He will have assignments he isn't crazy about and you need to be his cheerleader and hype girl.
5. Seniority in police departments is similar to the military, so prepare for him to spend time paying his dues.
6. At times he'll be called in on scheduled days off. He *has* to go, even if it means canceling family plans. Even big plans.

My biggest "aha" discovery: When your officer hubby knows he has a safe, resentment-free house to come home to every day, he will become the best version of himself.

A Great Attitude in a Police Marriage Will Make You Both Stronger

As my husband puts it, "The city owns me. They have almost complete control of my life." He goes on to say, "… when I go in, when I can take time off, when there is mandatory overtime, I *must* take part in it."

- **Attitude is everything:** When your officer comes home, do you check your attitude? Are you happy to see him, and does he see it on your face and in your body language? Are you careful not to show obvious disappointment that he had to sleep while you went to an event without him, one you originally planned to attend together?
- **Let him have his man cave:** Do you allow your man to have his space when he needs it? If he stays late after his shift to decompress with the guys, do you flow with it? He occasionally needs that time; it doesn't discredit you. Just like we women need girl time, guys need their guy time.
- **Jealousy:** Do you check your jealousy meter? This really needs a chapter all its own. It's truly a myth that most police marriages end in divorce. Most of my fellow police wives are still married to their officers after years and years. Keep communication open and set high expectations for each other. You will each live up to those expectations.

Police Tip 2
What to Expect as a Police Wife Through the Years

Once you establish flow and trust with each other, life as a police wife does get easier over time. I promise you it does.

1. Put full faith and trust in your hubby's professional police training. He will be able to tackle whatever dangerous situation that comes his way. *Believe.*
2. Have faith that God is watching over him and will bring him home safely to you and your kids (if you have them), each and every day.
3. It takes a strong, resilient woman to marry the man of her dreams and then be alone most days. But that's YOU! You are adaptable. You may often have completely different schedules and even if you have similar ones, late arrests or overtime may cause him to sleep most of the time when he is home. It's important and okay; you can handle it!
4. As the years go on, assignments change and your officer will gain seniority; therefore, he will generally get the vacation time and days off he puts in for. That is something to look forward to! This is when it starts getting easier.

Create Your Happy Place

Now that you have more knowledge about police family life and you know everything will get better over time, try these ideas:

- Keep doing hobbies that fill *you* up.
- Start new hobbies that excite you.
- Always maintain your girlfriend tribe; plan and DO fun things with them!
- Find fun things to do with your kids that Daddy isn't as crazy about. That way, you're guilt-free if/when he misses out.
- Find fun things to do just for YOU! Plan a spa day, take a dance class, schedule gym time, or get your nails done.
- Plan date nights yourself once in a while, instead of relying on him to always plan them. Be proactive!
- Plan short getaways once a year to keep the marriage fun and the spark alive.
- Start your own side business for extra money so you won't feel guilty about using "family money" to do the fun things you like and want to do.

Remember, when you practice "self-care", you can then give, give, give back to your husband and family! You can't be a GIVER when your tank is empty, so set aside time for things that keep your tank full.

*Notice how many times I said FUN above! Marriage and family life should be fun!

Police Tip 3
How You Can Best Support Your Police Hubby and Feel Supported by Him

Be a good listener.

1. Ask him about his day before you unload your day on him.
2. Be genuinely interested in the stories he tells you about his day (you will find them entertaining and fascinating).
3. When he feels "heard" he will be more open to listening to and meeting your needs. Hint, hint!

Have weekly or monthly and yearly goal-setting sessions together. Be a good communicator.

1. Plan your calendars together, going over upcoming events for the whole family. Keep a family calendar in the kitchen so both of you can easily update it. Have a digital family calendar too so you each can access and update when not at home.
2. Always discuss finances openly. Do not keep money secrets.
3. Hold dream-building sessions to make a five-year plan of what your life will look like, and update it yearly.
4. Have sex often. I repeat, have sex often! (Every husband will say this should be listed as number one.)

Relationships Are Always a Work in Progress, Especially in a Police Family

The pressure your husband is under day in and day out is truly like no other job anywhere in the world. Police are scrutinized from all sides: supervisors, the public, news media, social media, and sometimes even by friends and family. So, they definitely need your support more than most other humans on the planet.

- When he knows you understand him, when others criticize him, he will feel empowered to continue doing the right things in all areas of his life.
- Sharing a common faith and openly discussing your faith with your police hubby will bolster and support him.
- If your family or friends try to lump him in an inaccurate stereotype, you'd better set them straight. You know who he really is.
- Silence is okay. Sometimes men don't want to talk. They don't "need" to talk the way we women do. Respect that.
- When you need to talk about your day, but you just want to be heard and don't need him to "fix" things for you, be sure to make it clear: "I don't need/want you to fix anything, I just need to vent." That is the magic phrase that saves marriages.
- Keep humor alive **at all times**.

Police Tip 4
You Will Raise Incredible Children in Your Blue Family Using These Ideas

Raising kids in any family is tough, but just know they can and will thrive if you do it right!

Here are some possibly unconventional but impactful ideas that we used to raise two high school valedictorians who also played sports and volunteered in the community. Both graduated from UCLA and now lead active, thriving lives:

1. Read personal development books. (Contact me through my email or website and I'll offer you my favorites.)
2. Have your kids read personal development books too, starting as early as they can read. Audible is a great option for solidifying and retaining what they read.
3. Encourage them to do better than they did yesterday in school and in relationships. Have heartfelt talks often.
4. Be a coach, scout leader, PTA member, and contributor or at least be the 20% of parents who raise their hands to help at school and extracurricular activities.
5. Pick them up from school if at all possible and ask them about their day on the drive home. That is when they tell you everything!

Always Show Up and Be Present!

More unconventional ideas to implement:

- Do not give kids an allowance. Call it "earned money." They get a certain amount when each chore is completed.
- Each week set up three jars for the earned money: 10% goes to tithing (this can be considered donations), 20% goes to savings and the rest can be discretionary spending.
- Always meet the parents of the friends they play with, and especially before going to another child's house.
- Have real talks with your kids about trust and what happens when lies are told and how that will break your trust.
- Reward them by going on "real life" field trips to learn more about the world. On special occasions, allow them to miss school to see the world. If grades slip, they lose the privilege.
- Change your plans to show up at every possible event your kids participate in. We even went to sports practices. We didn't want to miss a thing, and we know how loved our kids felt!
- Apologize and take ownership for your own actions when you discover you were wrong or had a bad day and flew off the handle. (This is huge.) It shows them how they too should take responsibility when they are wrong. You will be leading by example in a big way.

Police Tip 5
Faith and Marriage Challenges

In police work, FAITH is not just needed—it is necessary. To us, this is non-negotiable. I am speaking to your police officer now:

1. There are so many bad guys who want to kill you, given the chance. You have to lean on a higher power to survive and go home to your family. Going alone can make you a dangerous cop.
2. In my opinion, put your faith first, your wife second, and the kids next to make it all work.

When you have marriage challenges, it is God you turn to, to ask for wisdom.

1. As a police couple, you each have your own personal relationship with God.
2. When you struggle with something, you may want to pray for God to show you what to do.
3. When my husband struggles, I pray and "give" him to God. I can't change my husband; he needs to change himself.
4. You may want to raise your kids to know that when they're nervous or scared about anything, a test, or their dad's safety, God will make them strong and carry them through. Never hesitate to talk to Him and ask for His help.

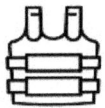

In a Police Marriage, Many Things Begin and End With Faith

Here are examples of typical disagreements and issues where you can turn to faith for help and guidance:

- Money issues
- Jealousy
- Night shifts
- Solo parenting
- Going to church without your spouse
- Household chores
- Working holidays
- Missing school functions
- Hanging out with partners after a shift
- Maintaining your girlfriend time

I highly recommend joining a Bible study with other police wives, or wives in general. There are so many biblical books and passages that are sources of inspiration and strength in times of trouble.

Here are just a few favorite books and verses from the Bible to refer to often:

Book of Romans
Book of Ruth
Philippians 4:8
Proverbs 31:10-31 "The wife of noble character"

Police Tip 6
Understanding How the World Sees Your Husband

Most civilians do not understand why we don't announce to the world that our husband is a police officer. "He works for the city" is my go-to answer if someone asks me.

1. Officer safety is the #1 reason families don't announce to everyone what their officer does for a living.
2. Officers' families don't live in the same city they work in for that very reason. They could be at the movies with their family and some bad guy they arrested sees them and follows them home.
3. People make judgments about police officers right away without treating them like human beings.
4. Also, for the safety of personal friends, it's wise to keep that quiet when going out in public.

Good news about off-duty police officers:

1. As a bystander, you will most likely be protected if something bad goes down; the officer can step in and save the day.
2. Off-duty officers usually have a weapon on their person for protection.

Most Civilians DO See Our Husbands in a Good Light

Thank goodness there are smart people in this world who understand a few bad apples don't make up nor do they contaminate the whole orchard. I was so happy when I discovered that most people appreciate police officers.

- Most people in this world are good people and see the good in others.
- Most people don't believe the rhetoric about "all cops are bad cops."
- Most people are true, law-abiding citizens with a strong moral compass.
- Most people know in their hearts that police officers sacrifice so much just to be out there protecting them from harm.

But with all that said, it is never safe to become complacent. Complacency is taboo in police work, and police families should definitely guard against it. So, in order to stay safe:

- Always be observant of your surroundings.
- Walk confidently and with purpose wherever you go, so you're not preyed upon by a criminal or criminals.
- Bad people are out there; don't be fooled into thinking bad things can't or won't happen to you.

Police Tip 7
Educating Friends and Family About Important Safety Concerns

In restaurants or any other public rooms, please let your officer friend pick a seat that does not place his back to the door. He needs to see who is entering so he can protect everyone.

Regarding the proud police friend/family member topic, most police officer families and friends are *not* aware that they should refrain from telling everyone in the room, specifically in public places, what the officer does for a living.

1. They are justifiably proud of their officer, and they want the world to know who they are and what they do for a living.
2. At the same time, they are clueless about how that disclosure could affect the officer's safety and his family's safety.

Here's an example you may relate to. My father was in the military and very proud that his son-in-law was a police officer. He told his whole Rotary club, all his friends, and every server in every restaurant, and flight attendants on every plane. We had to carefully and sweetly but firmly, ask him to stop.

Here's WHY You Don't Tell the Room

You may be asking yourself *why not?* Why would you ask them to stop sharing? You might even be thinking, "I would do the same. I really respect police officers and feel safer when one is nearby, so why wouldn't others feel the same and want to know?"

As I mentioned in the previous chapter, not all people have good intentions. With or even without the use of technology, bad things can happen quickly. Unfortunately, off-duty police officers are often targets for hate crimes.

As a civilian, you aren't trained to recognize known gang attire the way officers are trained to notice. You can't effectively determine if other people in the room within earshot of your conversations are good or bad, or if they are associated with bad people. Therefore, it is necessary to take common-sense precautions.

- Always keep your voice down. (This is hard for me because I talk loudly, ha ha.)
- Don't publicly announce what your officer does for a living.
- Keep a close circle of friends that you trust with that important and sensitive knowledge.
- Let your officer protect you by giving him the seat that faces the door.

Police Tip 8
What the World Doesn't Know About Your Husband

Public opinion of police and law enforcement in general seems to change by the decade and goes in cycles. Just like in the 1960s, right now as I write this book public sentiment has declined again. Before the COVID-19 pandemic, but especially during it, public opinion of police officers hit a serious all-time low.

It truly hurts the heart of a police wife who knows what we know about our husbands yet aren't able to shout it from the mountain tops for all the reasons I shared in Police Tip 7. So, I'd love to set the record straight here with these key points for you to consider:

1. Police officers choose law enforcement as a career because they truly want to *help people*. That is not to be taken lightly. They "choose," and know they will be in harm's way on a daily basis, protecting complete strangers because they believe God has led them to this calling.
2. They run toward danger when civilians are running *away*. Other first responders do not enter the scene UNTIL the police have arrived and neutralized the threat. Let that truly sink in.

Here's Something Quick-To-Judge Civilians Never Think About

Most crimes that are caught on video do not capture the crime in its entirety. To the naked eye of someone without law enforcement training, it can definitely look like police are overly aggressive, hurting "innocent" people who haven't done anything wrong.

Most of the time (99.99%), the officers are justified in their actions. Here's what a layperson can miss:

- The suspect punches an innocent bystander before the video starts rolling.
- The suspect brandishes a weapon before the video starts recording.
- The suspect intimidates store patrons and threatens their lives.
- The suspect commits crimes at different locations and flees the scene, winding up in a confrontation with the officers at the new location.

I could go on and on. If you're a civilian reading this book and trying to understand police life with an open mind, consider these final points.

- You don't ever have the full story by watching snippets on *any* news media outlet.
- Don't be quick to judge if you don't have all the facts.

Police Tip 9
Surviving Night and Overtime Shifts

It is common knowledge that most violent crimes are committed at night. Equipped with that knowledge, many police officers who want to do their best and make the most impact helping society work the night shift.

My husband chose to work the night shift when given the option to pick his shift. Our kids were three and four when Daddy decided to switch from business owner to police officer at 30 years old. Here are my favorite tips for the best sleep possible during daylight hours:

1. Buy blackout curtains.
2. Use a great noise-canceling app or play recorded beach waves to sleep by.
3. Have the kids eat/play/talk in the furthest room from the primary bedroom.
4. Teach the kids not to stomp their feet or shriek.
5. Reward your kids with their favorite things (toy/snack) if, for a whole week, they're quiet when Daddy sleeps.
6. Have a special routine for when Daddy wakes up, like bringing him a drink and listening to his stories about work from the night before.
7. Find a great sleep/circadian rhythm supplement and have him take it daily.

How Do You Help Kids Deal With Daddy Working So Much?

This is probably the hardest part, because of the compounded effect. Whether it's the opposite work hours of the family or the extra overtime shifts that most officers pick up to make ends meet, wives and kids get very sad when they can't see and spend time with their officer. Just like sleep deprivation, lack of quality time compounds emotionally day after day after day. Here are some things I suggest doing:

- Have a great attitude in front of your kids. Always support your husband's choice of shifts because many times he doesn't get to choose until he has seniority.
- Pay attention to your kids' attitudes. If you see discipline issues appearing, communicate them to your hubby. Most of our issues were solved by Daddy spending more quality time, especially with our son. He just needed more one-on-one Daddy time.
- Schedule lots of play dates with your kids' friends.
- Do things you like to do with your kids. You'll have a better attitude. For me, it was roller skating at the park and movie matinees.
- Talk favorably about what Daddy does, reiterating how much he helps other families by protecting them from crime.

Police Tip 10
Surviving the Most Important Family Holidays Without Him

"The city owns me." Remember that phrase from Tip 1? It perfectly describes how many officers feel about their lives, especially after multiple years on the job. When you're hired on, you're low man on the totem pole, even if you lateral over from another department. You still have to pay your dues, just like most jobs. Therefore, on major holidays like Christmas and New Year's Eve, your officer will have to work.

Here are suggestions for helping your officer's mental state:

1. Don't complain repeatedly about him not getting the day off.
2. Put a big smile on your face and give him a huge hug when he has to leave for work and when he comes home.
3. Reassure him that you or you and the kids are fine and that you will miss him, of course, and that *you've got this!*
4. Make a special treat for him to have at work and put a sweet note in the bag or lunch box (kids love helping here).

The #1 thing your officer wants to know is that his family is safe and HAPPY. Don't be a nag.

Here Are Suggestions for *Your* Well-Being

While I'm focusing a lot about caring for your officer, please understand that I deeply know the importance of *your* needs being met as well. I learned the hard way that it's unhealthy for any police wife to put their husband and children always first (after God) and completely forget about themselves. I did that in the beginning, and it did not serve me well.

You do need to recharge your batteries! You need to practice self-care as much as you build up your husband and kids. NEVER forget that!

Here are some things to do for YOU. This can be on a different day than the actual holiday, and that's okay. After all, you have a job to do on the holiday too. *Supermom* is your new name!

- Book a spa day for yourself.
- Go shopping *alone*.
- Get your nails done.
- Book a lunch date with your best girlfriend.
- Go to the movies alone (so you can finally see the movie you really want to see).
- Take up a new hobby.
- Start your own side business that has an awesome built-in community.

You can't take care of others if you don't take care of YOU!

Police Tip 11
How to Stop Feeling at Times Like a Divorcee

You can definitely feel like a divorcee in public, and also feel like you are the *only one* going through this dilemma. This is a very important topic, because I don't think there is a police wife out there who hasn't felt the sting of this emotion. If you don't have a lot of police wife friends in your immediate circle, you can also feel like you are totally on your own and that no one understands you, so you don't talk about it to anyone. Just know we do understand. You are not alone.

Let's just be real. Understanding the "conditions of the game" makes living it so much easier to handle:

1. You *will* fly Solo with the kids to multiple birthday parties in one day where everyone else has their husband by their side.
2. Attending church on Sundays, alone with the kids, becomes a normal event.
3. You will feel lonely.
4. Sometimes other men will hit on you, thinking you are a single mom.
5. Sometimes you will become resentful of your husband's job.

So, What Do You Do When You Feel Like "Ms. Divorcee?"

First of all, this is a real issue, but there's no sense "hanging" in your feelings and comparing yourself to others. It is what it is; you can't change it. Considering it "conditions of the game" make navigating your new normal easier.

- Definitely don't hold your feelings in. COMMUNICATE with your husband.
- Make a strategy together.
- Try to find places and times you can do things together (like couples' groups at church that might have better time slots to fit both of your schedules).
- Recognize that there will still be lots of events that he cannot attend with you. (Don't complain; it doesn't help. He would change it if he could.)
- Plan events around his schedule and invite friends to come to your place. (You know your officer is tired of driving places anyway.)
- Ask family and friends to give you as much notice as possible so he can ask for the day off (a huge help!) or switch days off if he is able.

Keep in mind always: *this too shall pass.* Just like every stage of life, the police job has stages. He will gain more seniority and be able to put in for those special days off. Pro tip: see if your officer can join a specialized unit; they usually get most holidays off.

Police Tip 12
Leveraging a Side Business to Reclaim Your Officer's Time

Have you ever pondered the idea of owning your own business alongside what you already do? John and I were entrepreneurs with a successful automotive accessory store way before he became a police officer. We know the value of tapping into a job and a business at the same time. We currently have a successful business that initially bought John's time back, enabling him to work less OT and then retire nine years earlier than planned. We dug the well before we needed the water. So why not start a side business yourself?

1. The tax code was written to benefit business owners (check with your tax professional) not employees.
2. You can write off many things as a business owner that you can't write off as an employee.
3. If you pick the right business, you can work it alongside what you already do.

What business is best to start? Look for a consumable products business where people buy the product, use it up, need more, and buy again. Look for a product line in a rich and evergreen space with mentors willing to help you build. Reach out to me if you'd like my advice. We have researched so many and found *THE ONE*.

How Do You Find the Right Business?

This is the million-dollar question, or in today's world, it's the billion-dollar question. So many people try and fail at business, so it makes novices in this arena afraid to even start. In my opinion, you need to seek guidance from an expert who has a business and is already where you want to be in life. In other words, you don't want to take advice from your broke neighbor, co-worker, or family. Best advice: seek out trusted advisors.

- Be open to starting a business even if "business" scares you and is out of your comfort zone.
- Be open to something that isn't a passion of yours, contrary to what many people try to tell you.
- Use common sense in your decision-making.
- Be open to things that *sell* vs. things you think people should want to have.

After you have discussed your plans with your trusted advisor ...

- Weigh the pros and cons of the business.
- Discuss with your spouse, but if you feel strongly and your spouse does not agree, be strong and own your choice after debating the pros and cons.
- Decide, act on it, and don't look back.
- Give it 100% like you give to your job; it will pay you back tenfold.

Police Tip 13
How to Build Up Your Husband When the Job Begins to Tear Him Down

This is probably a given, but it is worth reading again and again: a positive supportive happy home life is critical to your officer's mental state. He wants that, he craves it, and when job pressures, supervisors, and outside influences like the media keep piling on, you can be a buffer for him to feel heard, loved, understood and respected.

What is the best way to make that happen?
(Should I say, SEX again? But seriously ...)

1. When he shares work stories, be all ears. Pay attention and be involved.
2. Pick up the slack at home like fixing things, doing yard work, taking out trash, even if those are all "his" jobs.
3. Make Google and YouTube your best friends to teach yourself new skills with "how to" videos.
4. Don't complain that you're doing more at home than he is (he will see everything you're doing and do more to help out than if you simply nag him about it).
5. Compliment him on how he looks, but most importantly, on a job well done at work. Lord knows he won't be hearing it from most supervisors or the world.

Limit Exposure to Negative Sources

Mainstream media sensationalizes what it reports. Gone are the days of unbiased journalism. When you watch the news, they grab your attention with the worst story of the day, and then another bad story, rarely showing the good side of humanity. I could write an entire book on this subject. So, what do you do?

First, here are some don'ts:

- Don't leave the TV on with a news channel playing 24/7.
- Don't listen to criticism of the police, even if you're trying to prove your point about the media to friends or family.
- Don't try to watch a "police drama" with your husband. He will point out every incorrect tactic, or how the writers got it wrong because in reality police work would never be done the way the show portrays it. Save your sanity.

Instead try these ideas, the dos:

- Listen to a great life or couple-affirming podcast together, preferably a funny one. Humor helps you vent.
- Pick a book to read at the same time and discuss each chapter. (Contact me for my fave books to read together.)
- Choose uplifting shows to watch.
- Read the Bible together; share *aha* moments or epiphanies!

Police Tip 14
Prioritizing Your Buddy and Girlfriend Time

As mentioned earlier, I was originally hurt and upset that my husband chose to stay after work and meet up with his fellow officer buddies after working with them all night. I would selfishly think, "Good grief, hasn't he seen them enough already," and, "Hey, what about me?"

Some valuable lessons learned:

1. Patrol officers don't work in a cubical.
2. They definitely don't hang out with the guys in their unit all night. Two officers share a car; they answer radio calls all throughout their shift.
3. After their shift, decompressing and debriefing their police work is best done when the main "brass" is not around.

So, what do they do when they hang out?

1. They share different capers that happened and their outcomes.
2. They discuss tactics and how to improve on the next incident.
3. Younger officers learn a lot when they share off-the-record debriefings with their watch partners.

The Main Point Behind Buddy Time May Not Be What You Think

The key point is that your officer surrounds himself with coworkers who can be open and honest with each other. They battle every day for their lives. They want to safely come home to you and also not bring negativity back to the family. The buddy time is very much like opening a pressure release valve. It truly lets them vent, blow off steam, and stay mentally healthy for you and the kids. It's a very effective practice, one I'm glad to finally appreciate. So, just let him go and do his thing!

So, what's this about girlfriend time?

I also learned some valuable lessons about girlfriend time. In a police family, you definitely need to keep your girlfriends close. It's easy to think non-police friends won't understand what you're going through, but that's not why you need them. You need them for all the reasons every wife needs her girlfriends.

- You can talk and talk and talk; they don't tune you out.
- Your girlfriends are your hype squad and vice versa.
- Your girlfriends see the world differently than your hubby does.
- Our feminine side always feels protected and supported by like femininity.
- We girls need to vent too!

Police Tip 15
Fulfilling Your Dreams Before And During Retirement

Retirement is what most people look forward to! But planning starts well before retirement. Thank goodness most departments have great retirement counselors and if they don't, start investigating for yourself. It seems crazy to start planning for retirement right when your hubby gets hired on, but it's the smartest thing you will ever do. Here are some retirement planning tips:

1. Seek out a financial advisor who preferably has firsthand knowledge of the unique police officer lifestyle (we found a great one and can recommend them).
2. Along with planning for retirement, create your kids' college fund even if they haven't been born yet.
3. Seriously consider starting a side business as shared in Tip 12. Dig the well before you need the water—this is key!
4. Hold regular monthly financial planning meetings with your hubby to keep your budget on track.
5. Each year choose something from your dream board and make it come true. This keeps you hyped for what's to come! Don't have extra $$$ to do that? Start that side business and watch yourself create the money you need.

Retirement Doesn't Have to Be for Old People

If you plan properly and reward yourself along the way, you will be making your dreams come true, now and in the future, to live fulfilled.

John and I did all the things I have shared in these 15 police tips and we are ecstatic about our life. We never listened to the haters and naysayers, and you shouldn't either. By following these tips and treating them as a mini course, your life will become all that you dreamed it would be when you were dating and talking about what you wanted for the future.

We are truly living the life of our dreams now. At the young age of 55, John retired early after 25 years on the job. You can even do it at a younger age if that's what you desire. I dare you. In fact, I double dare you!

- It's time for good people like you to be rewarded for your efforts.
- It's time for you to believe that all things are possible.
- If other people can have massive success in life, so can YOU!
- It's time to *believe in yourself* and know that you are WORTHY.
- Don't believe that dreams are silly because dreams do come true. They have come true for us, and we want to help you make yours come true too!

You've finished. Before you go …

Post/Share that you finished this book.

Please star rate this book.

Reviews are solid gold to writers. Please take a few minutes to give us some itty bitty feedback.

ABOUT THE AUTHOR

Vikki Downey is a powerful leader with a diverse background in entrepreneurship, education, and mentorship. Vikki graduated from UC Irvine with a Bachelor of Arts degree in dance. While at UCI, she actively engaged in many leadership roles, including Pi Beta Phi chapter president, and after college dedicated herself to community service as a Girl Scout leader and became leader of the year.

Vikki's entrepreneurial journey began as the co-owner of Prestige Motoring Accessories, Inc. with her husband John. The Downeys ran that successful business in the city of Brea, CA for 10 years before John decided to become a police officer with the Los Angeles Police Department.

As a proud police wife, Vikki has found her niche in inspiring other police wives to bring additional income into their families. She is dedicated to helping them reduce the need for their husbands to work excessive overtime gigs just to make ends meet. Alongside her husband John, she has developed a plan to assist other police families by helping their officers retire early by leveraging the extra income generated from their own online businesses.

With a deep passion for mentorship, education, entrepreneurship, and supporting police families, Vikki is committed to empowering individuals and driving positive change. Her expertise and dedication make her a valuable resource in the online business space.

If you enjoyed this Itty Bitty™ book you might also like…

- **Your Amazing Itty Bitty™ Awaken the Leader Within** – Natalie Clayton

- **Your Amazing Itty Bitty™ Family Leadership Book** – Jacqueline T. D. Huynh

- **Your Amazing Itty Bitty™ Business Tax Book** – Deborah A. Morgan

Or any of the many Amazing Itty Bitty™ books available online at
www.ittybittypublishing.com

www.ingramcontent.com/pod-product-compliance
Lightning Source LLC
Chambersburg PA
CBHW061306040426
42444CB00010B/2538